THE OWL & THE CRAGRAT

THE OWL & THE CRAGRAT

Climbs and Rhymes

An anthology of climbing poetry

Edited by Marc Chrysanthou and Gordon Stainforth

Illustrated by Duncan Bourne

AURELIUS

First published in Great Britain in 2004
by Stonegold Publishing
15 Stubbing Square, Hebden Bridge HX7 6LT
www.stonegold.co.uk

Aurelius is an imprint of Stonegold Publishing
(in association with The Hyacinth's Authors' Front)

A proportion of the proceeds from this book will go to

the brain injury association

Registered charity number 1025852
www.headway.org.uk

Project Director: Gordon Stainforth

Design, typesetting and digital artwork by
Nick Alcock: www.nickalcock.com

ISBN 0-9547107-0-3

Printed in England by
Antony Rowe Ltd
Chippenham, Wiltshire

Contents

FOREWORD

The poems in this anthology are reproduced, with some amendments, from poems contributed by users of Rocktalk (www.ukclimbing.com/forums, an on-line chat forum for climbers in December 2003). Initially, I conceived the idea of adapting W.B. Yeats' 'An Irish Airman Foresees His Death' and turning it into a poem about a solo climber having a premonition of his doom. This original act of 'creative plagiarism' immediately spawned many others, and, within a period of just two weeks, nearly two hundred 'adaptations' had been submitted by forum users (the original thread can be visited at www.ukclimbing.com/forums/t.php?t=66319). This volume contains many of these offerings.

I prefer to call these poems and songs 'adaptations' rather than 'parodies' because the latter term conveys a sense of poking fun at or exploiting the originals, which I feel is (largely!) absent. Reading the adapted poems, one senses a love of the original poetry and a careful attention to the metre and rhyme of the original verses. Thus, whilst the 'new' poems stand as poems in their own right, they also pay subtle homage to the original authors' imaginations and skill. Thankfully, the majority of the original poets are no longer with us (though none, as far as I am aware, died in a climbing mishap), so, unlike chippers of real rock, the chippers of the marble of classic poetry are fairly safe from threat of personal harm or legal action (though Shelley or Blake may be turning in their graves somewhere on Mount Helicon or the Elysian Fields, or wherever it is that dead poets go).

As the 'author' of many of these poems I can attest to the addictive nature of this act of creative alteration. Indeed, several of the contributors are, as I write, receiving treatment for PAOCS (Poem Altering Obsessive-Compulsive Syndrome) at a clinic high in the Alps – an unfamiliar terrain of three-dimensional mountains, far removed from their home in the virtual reality hills of Flatscreenland. The contributors have obviously had great fun moulding the original clay to fit their new designs. In certain instances, the adapted poems feel uncannily 'right' – almost as though they had originally been conceived as poems about climbing. In some parallel postmodern universe surely 'I wandered once up to Hen Cloud, that floats on high o'er Staffordshire's hills' and 'Wobbliest of knees, my left knee now' are the originals and Wordsworth and Housman but pale imitations. In other cases, the original poem's tone has been ingeniously subverted – creating incongruities of tone, style and meaning that may be, by turns, unsettling and amusing. The enjoyment of all the poems and lyrics presented in this compilation is enhanced greatly by reading them side-by-side with the originals.

The contributions have been grouped into themes exemplifying a particular aspect of climbing: e.g. Equipment, Camaraderie, Death, Fear, Bouldering and Nostalgia.

Accordingly, the poems can be read thematically. Alternatively, the reader may simply dip his or her chalk-coated fingers in at random. There is enough variety of original authors, styles and themes to suit poetry-loving boulderers, sports climbers or bumblies. So here it is then! Feel free to clip the book to your harness – to while away hours spent on belay ledges awaiting dawdling seconds.

We hope you enjoy it – but the best tribute we could be accorded is if, whilst leading some gritstone slab one idyllic autumn day, inspiration strikes, and you find yourself mentally composing your own 'original' poem ... *'If I should die think only this of me; that there is some corner of some ... gritstone edge ...* Hah! Nice one! ... *that is forever ...* Hmmm, what word can I use instead of 'England'? Newlands? Portland? ... Wilton? ... What's that, Derek?! My runners have all come out?! Look, don't bother me now, I'm writing a poem ... O God, I'm off! ... Aaaaaargh!'

Marc Chrysanthou, January 2004

In the Beginning

---❖---

The poem that started the (chalk)ball rolling ...

A Solo Climber Foresees His death
(based on W.B.Yeats' 'An Irish Airman Foresees His Death')

———◆●◆———

I KNOW that I shall meet my fate,
Somewhere among the crags above;
Those back at home will think me late,
Until their fears inflame their love;
My 'country' is Snowdonia's heights,
My 'countrymen' the ghostly sheep,
No shattered end would bring delight
Or cause their muffled hearts to weep.
Nor friends, nor duty bade me climb,
No well-thumbed guides, nor cheering crowds;
A lifetime's seeking the sublime
Led to this meeting in the clouds.
I teetered left, becalmed my mind;
The route ahead dispelled my breath;
No way above, no way behind,
Fingers once clasped to Life, touched Death.

Marc Chrysanthou

THE CLIMBING EXPERIENCE

Last night I dreamed that it was possible to sample the experiences of all climbers (all 465,232 of them) and splice them together into an intricate overlapping mosaic – a kaleidoscope of memories, emotions and achievements. I looked through this kaleidoscope and, Oh, the experience was dazzling, awe-inspiring, heart-stopping, terrifying, vertigo-inducing!... Or maybe I'd simply drunk too much Special Brew the night before ...

GRIT FEVER
(based on John Masefield's 'Sea-Fever')

————◆●◆————

I MUST go out to the Peak again, the lonely Peak on high,
And all I ask is a gritstone slab and a bouldering mat nearby,
And the slipper smear and the sidepull and the crystal pinch biting,
And a clear day and a cold day and the clean boot striking.

Simon Jones

CHALK FEVER
(based on John Masefield's 'Sea-Fever')

————◆●◆————

I MUST dip my hands in the chalkbag again,
Although they're quite bone dry,
I get this affliction now and then,
Can anyone tell me why?

Nick Alcock

'I JAM ...'
(based on John Clare's 'I am')

I JAM: yet, when I jam, it stays then goes ...
My Friends forsake me, my protection's lost;
I am the self-consumer of my woes –
   I rise, relapse to my precarious post,
Like a hippo in its frenzied death throes –
And yet, I hang on ! like a ship storm-tossed.

Out of the cosiness of the pub's noise,
   Into the reality of silent screams,
Where there is neither sense of hope nor joys,
   But the vast shipwreck of my armchair dreams;
Even the first pitch – that should give no test –
Is hard – nay, rather harder than the rest.

I long for holds, the biggest made by God,
   A jug whose size would make me feel much blessed –
Then turn to smile at my belayer, Rod,
   And leap as I in wild dreams deftly leapt:
Unflustered – on the front cover of *High*;
The fear below – above, the vaulted sky.

Marc Chrysanthou

A CLIMBER'S PRAYER

(based on A.A. Milne's, 'When We Were Very Young': 'Vespers')

———◆•◆———

LITTLE Boy kneels at the foot of the crag,
Drops on the ground his little rope bag.
Hush! Hush! Whisper who dares!
Another climber is saying his prayers.

God bless gritstone. I know that's right.
So much fun, I could climb all night.
The cracks are so cracky, and the grit's so grit!
Oh! *God bless Limestone* – it's not that sh*t.

If I open my fingers a little bit more,
I can see my gear bag, just there on the floor.
It's a beautiful gear bag, but it hasn't a zip.
Oh! *God bless my quickdraws, may they always clip.*

Oh! *Thank you, God, for a beautiful day.*
And what was the other I had to say?
I said 'Bless Limestone', so what can it be?
Oh! Now I remember it. *God bless Me.*

Little boy kneels at the foot of the crag,
Drops on the ground his little rope bag.
Hush! Hush! Whisper who dares!
Another climber is saying his prayers.

Amanda James

HURT

(based on Trent Reznor's lyrics to the song 'Hurt')

———◆•◆———

I HURT myself today
In seeking friction's feel
I focus on the climb
the only thing that's real
Tore a finger on a hold
That old familiar sting
I tried to lay-away
but I couldn't stop the swing

What do I care now
My belay friend
everyone I know
Falls off in the end
and I want to climb it all
This empire of Grit
If I hit the ground
It is sure to hurt

I wear an old helmet
upon my thinning hair
I'm full of aching bones
that took ages to repair
but on these rocks sublime
the feelings disappear
I am somewhere else
I am without fear

Chorus

If I slip again
and my hand peels away
I will get back on
I will find a way

Duncan Bourne

THE VOICE (ON THE CRAGS)
(based on Rupert Brooke's 'The Voice')

SAFE in the magic of the crag
I climbed, above the dying light.
Faint in the pale high solitudes,
  Of rock cleansed with rain and veiled by night,

Silver and blue and green were showing.
  And the dark grew darker still;
And birds were hushed; and peace was growing;
  And quietness crept up the hill;

And no wind was blowing

And I knew
That this was the hour of knowing,
And the night and the moves and you
Were one together, and I should find
Soon in the silence the hidden key
Of all that had hurt and puzzled me –
Why you were you, and the night was kind,
And the rock was part of the heart of me.

And there I clung breathlessly,
Alone; and slowly the holy three,
The three that I loved, together grew
One, in the hour of knowing,
Night, and the climb, and you –

And suddenly
There was an uproar above the route,
The noise of a fool in mock distress,
Crashing and laughing and blindly going,
Of ignorant feet and a clanging hex,
And a Voice profaning the solitudes.
The spell was broken, the key denied me

And at length your flat clear voice beside me
Mouthed cheerful clear flat platitudes.

You came and quacked above me on the crag.
You said, 'The view from here is very good!'
You said, 'It's nice to be alone a bit!'
And, 'How the days are drawing out!' you said.
You said, 'The sunset's pretty, isn't it?'

* * * * *

By God! I wish – I wish that you were dead!

Paul Saunders

DIARY OF A GRIT MOUSE

(based on Sir John Betjeman's 'Diary of a Church Mouse')

— ● —

HERE among long-ascended classics,
Damp chimneys, and half-open 'jam cracks',
Here where the bolter never looks
I work my way through old guide books.
Lean and alone I spend my days
Behind this dreary Peak District haze.
The weather never bothers me,
So here I eat my frugal tea.

  Summer and Easter may be great
For limestone, granite and for slate,
And so may Whitsun. All the same,
They do not support my meagre frame.
For me the only feast at all
Is Autumn's Friction Festival,
When I can satisfy my want
With smears of joy (just like in 'Font').
I climb each gritstone greasy runnel
To burrow through 'Helfenstein's Struggle'.
I scramble up 'Appointment with Fear'
And laugh aloud while hanging there.

  It is enjoyable to taste
These routes before they go to waste,
But how annoying when one finds
That other folks with simple minds
Come to the Peaks my crags to share
Who have no proper business there.
Two outdoor groups with no desire
To be lead at all, attract my ire.
A rambler (who clearly is a prat)
Comes over to see what I am at.
He says 'The Ouzels soon will nest …
'You'd best come down, it's for the best'.
This year he blocked access for weeks

(I'd like to kick him 'in the Peaks'),
And prosperous men from London way
Come in SUVs and stay all day,
And wearing all the latest gear,
Fill cracks with Friends to stave off fear.
A 'low traverser' thinks that I
Am traditional and climb too high,
Yet somehow doesn't think it wrong
To top rope Great Slab for far too long,
While I, who stay the whole year through,
Must share my crag with climbers who
Except at this time of the year
Not once upon the rock appear.
   Within the climbing world I know
Such goings-on should not be so,
For *proper* Climbers' only do
What their pure ethics tell them to.
They read their route guides every day
And always, night and morning, train,
And just like me, of Gritstone stock,
Worship each week on 'God's Own Rock',
   But all the same it's strange to me
How very full the crags can be
With *boulderers* I don't see at all
Except on Tuesday at the wall.

Paul Saunders

*The true climber is not someone who feels no fear. No. Someone
without fear is a robot, an automaton of the rock, or else an idiot.
The true climber is someone who feels fear, summons his deepest
resources of courage, coolness and self-discipline – and then calls
for a toprope.*

IF

(based on Rudyard Kipling's 'If')

IF you can keep your head when all about you
   Are losing theirs and blaming it on you,
If you can trust yourself when inner whispers doubt you,
   Because years of mental training's taught you to;
If you can lead and not be tired of leading,
   Or being second, never criticize,
Or fearing falling, don't give in to failure,
   Yet don't deal in idle boasts, nor talk too wise:

If you can smear – and not make slabs your master;
   If you can crimp – and not make walls your bane;
If you can lead on Rhyolite and Gritstone
   And treat those two sediments just the same;
If you can bear to hear the gear you've put in
   Twisted by ropes, then come undone,
Or watch the bolt you banked your life on, broken,
   Shrug your shoulders and just carry on.

If you can make a leap to distant handholds
   And by such a dyno risk great loss,
And fall, and start again at the beginning
   And never blame wet holds or slimy moss;
If you can force your heart and nerve and sinew
   To crank long after they've cried 'Enough!',
And to hold on when there is nothing in you
   Except the Will which says to them: 'Hang tough!'

If you can wear tight lycra and keep your street-cred,
    Or pose for mags – nor lose the common touch,
If neither dreams of fame nor wealth can faze you,
    If all routes count with you, but none too much;
If you can brave the unforgiving mountain
    With sixty metres' worth of nine-mill line,
Yours are the heights and all the honour,
    And – much more – the title 'Climber' will be thine!

Marc Chrysanthou

WOBBLIEST OF KNEES
(based on A.E. Housman's 'Loveliest of Trees')

—◆●◆—

WOBBLIEST of knees, my left knee now
As I approach the holdless prow,
And the sweat pours from my hide
As my boot begins to slide.

Now I'm threescore years and ten,
Boldness will not come again,
And if courage wasn't there before,
I'll never feel the lion's roar.

And since to lead routes so smooth-hewn
Takes raw nerve and va-va-voom,
About the High Peak I will go
To *see* the climbs I'll never know.

Marc Chrysanthou

NASTYROCKY
(based on Lewis Carroll's 'Jabberwocky')

'TWAS chossy and the slimy stones
  Did crack and crumble down the face;
All flimsy were her borrowed ropes,
  And her old rack a disgrace.

'Beware the Nastyrock, my girl!
  The polished holds, no grip to get!
Beware the offwidth crack, and shun
  The ominous arête!'

She took her trusty guide in hand;
  Long time the manxome line she weighed –
So rested she by the bendy tree,
  And looked above, dismayed.

And as in uffish thought she paused,
  A nasty rock, that screamed Beware!
Came whistling down the bulgy wall,
  And missed her by a hair!

Left, right! Left, right! She scaled the height:
  Her rubber shoes went ticky tack!
She topped out fine, and claimed the line,
  Then went a'scrambling back.

'And hast thou climbed the Nastyrock?
  Come to my arms, my beamish lass!
O frabjous day! Callooh! Callay!'
  He chortled like an ass.

'Twas chossy and the slimy stones
  Did crack and crumble down the face;
All flimsy were her borrowed ropes,
  And her old rack a disgrace.

Marc Chrysanthou and Amanda James

THE WATCHERS

(based on Walter de la Mare's 'The Listeners')

———◆•◆———

'OK, watch me here,' said the Climber,
  Turning to his task once more;
While his dog wandered off hunting rabbits
  In the dusk falling over the tor:
And a bird flew out of the chimney,
  Above the Climber's head:
And he drove in the jams again a second time;
  'Definitely this time,' he said.
But no one responded to the Climber,
  No second on that heath-ringed hill
Looked up and tended any sturdy line
  While he hung, flexed, yet still.
But only a host of phantom watchers
  That gathered beneath him then:
Stood watching in the failing of the daylight
  With indifference to the fate of men:
Stood thronging the faint footholds in the dark there,
  And those quiet slabs and walls,
Alert now to the confidence shaken
  And the nervous Climber's call.

And he felt now the start of dread weakness,
  And knew that his sinews must try,
While his dog returned impatient,
  'Neath the blackening sky;
For he suddenly pulled once more, even
  Harder, and lifted his head: –
'It's OK, I know I can do this,
  And I'm on toprope,' he said.
Never the least stir made the watchers,
  Though every move he made
Felt unequal to the sketchiness of that steep wall

To that one man, now afraid:
Ay, they heard his foot roll off the step-up,
    And the sound of skin grasping stone,
And how the silence surged softly backward,
When the plunging fall was done.

Dave Garnett

A Cautionary Tale:
(based on Hilaire Belloc's 'A Cautionary Verse')

━━━◆◆━━━

The Chief Defect of Henry King
  Was, he could not climb anything.
No matter what Grade route he found
  He simply could not leave the Ground;
Or if he did, he quickly fell,
  And all around would hear him yell,
Until one day he found a Cliff
  (Whose hardest route was just V Diff)
Of well-protected, friendly Grit:
  Oh, how he longed to climb on it!
And so one Day he took his Sack,
  His Climbing Rope, his Boots, his Rack,
His Sandwiches, his little Flask,
  He was quite ready for the Task.
But just to make his Heart feel gladder
  He took along a little Ladder.

The other Climbers watched, amazed,
  As Henry King his Ladder raised;
And, while a deathly Silence hung,
  He climbed the Ladder, rung by rung.
Alas! his Plan it was a Flop –
  The Ladder didn't reach the Top!
He quickly felt the Ladder's Lack
  Of height, and wedged into Crack
A Friend (it was a Number Four),
  Then swiftly placed a couple more.
This gear so highly raised his Hope,
  He quite forgot to clip the Rope!
But all oblivious to this State,
  And unaware what was his Fate,
He laybacked off a Sharp Arête

(A better Hold you could not get);
And for the first, and Only, Time,
Henry King began to climb!

He handjammed boldly up a Crack,
  A Chimney led with Foot and Back;
Though tension heightened every Sense,
  He was so full of Confidence.
But as he dyno'd for the Top,
  A Voice below him shouted, 'Stop!
You Fool, you haven't clipped your Gear!'
  And Henry's Heart went cold with Fear.
He very soon began to quake,
  And both his Knees began to shake,
'Til from his Holds he nearly slipped –
  He was most definitely gripped!
Then, just as he was losing Hope,
  Somebody lowered him a Rope,
And would have saved him from his Fate,
  If they had not been just too late,
For Henry's Feet slipped from the Ledge,
  His Fingers uncurled from the Edge,
And with a most Blood-curdling Yell,
  Henry to the Bottom fell,
Almost from the very Top,
  And landed with a sort of 'Plop!'
All you who listen to my Tale,
  Be sure you never, ever fail
To clip your Gear when you do climb,
  Be sure you do it every Time!
But there is one more Lesson clear,
  For Climbers with the Sense to hear:
Always keep tight hold of Grit,
  For Fear of ending in the ...

Howard Jones

THE SHAKESPEAREAN SLAB CLIMBER'S SOLILOQUY
(based on William Shakespeare's 'Hamlet', Act 3, Sc 1)

To smear or not to smear; that is the question:
Whether 'tis nobler to decline, then suffer
The ribbings and goads of ungracious friends,
Or to place foot against a smeary knobble,
And, with thumb opposing, 'send' it? To try; to slip –
Not sure; and, by a slip to say we end
The calf-ache and the frowns and sweaty socks
That fear gives rise to – 'tis a resolution
Devoutly to be wished. To try, to slip;
To rip perchance the gear. Ay, there's the rub,
For in that slide of 'death' what screams may come
When we have shuffled off grit's mortal foil
Must give us pause. And then, if held,
There's the misery of a long life;
For who would bear the jokes and jeers of time,
The pisstaker's song, the hardman's contumely,
The harangues of onlookers, kids at play,
The insolence of walkers, and the quips
Impatient topropers, less worthy, make,
As he himself his quietude fakes
With a sheepish grin? Who would insults wear,
And grin and bear the 'Nearly Man' jibes,
If he lacked not the commitment to success
That taps the undiscover'd reservoir of faith
Slab climbers sup from, else muzzle their will;
And makes us rather bear those spills we have
Than 'go for it' and 'pull it off'?
Thus confidence's lack makes cowards of us all,
And thus the native glue of resolution

Is unstickied with the pale cast of doubt,
And ascents of greatness end the moment
Climbers allow sly doubts to multiply,
And lose the gain of friction.

Marc Chrysanthou

Two on a Rope

A rope has two ends. That simple fact is no accident. It is a physical statement of the symbolic bond of brotherhood (and sisterhood) that is forged whenever two questing spirits trust each other enough to link souls and destinies. But do try to avoid climbing with anyone with a less than rugged or 'climberly' name. Calling 'Climb when ready, Xavier!' can seriously damage your street- and rock-cred.

Your Long Lost Pal
(based on Paul Simon's 'You can call me Al')

———◆●◆———

A MAN climbs up a route
He says why is it soft in the middle now
Why am I soft in the middle
The rest of the route is so hard
I need a photo-opportunity
I want a shot in the magazines
Don't want to end up in a guidebook
In a guidebook, graveyard
Headpointer Headpointer
Bolts in the moonlight
Far away from my well-lit crag
Mr Beerbelly Beerbelly
Get these cams away from me
You know I don't find this stuff amusing any more

If you'll be my belayguard
I can be your long lost pal,
And Dinky when you call me
You can call me Al.

A man climbs up a rock
He says why am I short of protection
Got a short span of protection
And woe, my run out is long
Where's my girl and dog
What if I die here
Who'll be my role model
Now that my role model is
Gone, gone,
He ducked back down the
Crack, with some dodgy, dodgy, tatty kind of gear
All along there were incidents and accidents
There was bad gear and nasty placements

If you'll be my belayguard
I can be your long lost pal,
And Dinky when you call me
You can call me Al.

A man climbs a piece of rock
It's a rock in a strange world
Maybe it's a rock in the third world
He doesn't speak the language
He knows nothing of it
He's a foreign man
He is surrounded by the rock
The rock
Cattle in the marketplace
Scatterlings and orphanages
He looks around, around,
He sees angels in the rock formations
Spinning in infinity
He says Amen! And Hallelujah!

If you'll be my belayguard
I can be your long lost pal,
And Dinky when you call me
You can call me Al.

Nick Alcock

LOST

(based on AA Milne's 'Disobedience')

JAMES James
Morrison Morrison
Weatherby George Dupree
Took great
Care with his belay –
A rope wrapped around a tree.
James James said to his ropemate,
'Ropemate,' he said, said he;
'You must never ab down
To the ledge near the ground
If you don't first check with me.'

James James
Morrison's ropemate
Put on a serious frown
James James Morrison's ropemate
Said to herself said she;
'I *will* ab down
to the ledge near the ground
and climb back at about E3.'

Chris Bonington
Put up a notice,
LOST or STOLEN or STRAYED
JAMES JAMES MORRISON'S ROPEMATE
SEEMS TO HAVE BEEN MISLAID
LAST SEEN
DANGLING IN MID-AIR
WITHOUT A PRUSSIK CORD,
SHE TRIED TO AB DOWN
TO THE LEDGE NEAR THE GROUND –
FIFTY EUROS REWARD!'

James James
Morrison Morrison
(Commonly known as Jim)
Told all his
Climbing buddies
Not to go blaming him.
James James
Said to his ropemate
'Ropemate,' he said, said he;
'You must never ab down
To the ledge near the ground
If you don't first check with me.'

James James
Morrison's ropemate
Hasn't been heard of since
Bonners said he was sorry,
So did Big Ron and Joe Brown.
Bonners
(Somebody told me)
Said to a man he knew,
'If people ab down to a ledge near the ground, well,
What can anyone do?'

(Now then, very softly:)

J. J.

M. M.

W. G. Du P.

Took great

C/o his R*******

With a rope wrapped around a tree.

J. J.

Said to his ********

'R*******', he said, said he:

'You-mustn't-ab-down-to-the-ledge-near-the-ground-if-
you-don't-first-check-with-ME!'

Nick Alcock and Marc Chrysanthou

WHO CLIMBS WITH FERGUS?
(based on W.B. Yeats' 'Who Goes With Fergus?')

WHO will go climb with Fergus now,
And hold his rope on Javelin Blade,
And glance upon Llyn Idwal's shore?
Young man, lift up your furrowed brow,
And pay out the rope – once safe belayed,
Until the rope runs out no more.

And no more turn aside and brood
Upon his subtle mastery;
For Fergus rules the granite scars,
And rules the sky as red as blood,
And the white quartz of the loose scree
And all dishevelled wandering stars.

Marc Chrysanthou

THE MAN STOOD ON THE BELAY LEDGE
(based on Felicia Hemans' 'The Boy Stood on the Burning Deck')

THE man stood on the belay ledge
Whence all but he had fled;
The rain that lashed the seashore
Drummed down upon his head.

Yet beautiful and bright he stood,
As born to rule the zawn;
A creature of heroic blood,
A proud, though childlike form.

The rope roll'd up ... he would not go
Without his leader's word;
That leader, faint in clouds above,
His voice no longer heard.

He call'd aloud ... 'Say, leader, say
If yet thy task is done!'
He knew not that the leader lay
Unconscious of his chum.

'Speak, leader!' once again he cried,
'If I may yet be gone!'
And but the booming shouts replied,
And fast the world roll'd on.

Upon his prow he held his breath,
And tossed his waving hair,
And looked from that lone post of death,
In still yet brave despair;

And shouted but once more aloud,
'My leader, must I stay?'
While o'er him fast, through cloud and storm
The rope began to fray.

He leapt, his heart a beating wild,
As from upon a high,
Came streaming above the gallant child,
Rope tendrils in the sky.

There came a burst of thunder sound ...
The man – oh! where was he?
Ask of the winds that far around
With fragments strewed the sea.

With harness, helmet, and rock shoes fair,
That well had borne their part;
But the noblest thing which perished there
Was that young and faithful heart.

Darren Jackson

A Sick Climber's Confession

(based on William Carlos Williams' 'This is just to say')

I HAVE eaten
the Kendal Mintcake
that was in
your rucksack

and which
you were probably
saving
for the summit bid

Forgive me
I couldn't resist …
so sweet …
so bloody sickly …

yuck

Marc Chrysanthou

GEAR FREAKS

The main reason men (and some women) love climbing is that it provides an excuse for grown-ups to play with shiny, technical toys. This love of equipment is an unrequited love – those gleaming chocks and multicoloured ropes are blissfully unaware of our devotion; in fact, some of them are hell-bent on bringing about our deaths.

ROCKBOOT
(based on Sylvia Plath's 'Daddy')

———◆●◆———

YOU do not do, you do not do
Any more, black shoe
In which I have squashed my left foot
For three years, poor and white,
Barely daring to breathe or Achoo.

5.10 Diamond, I have had to bin you.
You died before I had topped out –
Gritstone-gripped, a bag full of chalk,
Still as a statue with one grey toe,
Big as a Leeds pigeon

Swollen with the constriction,
Gradually turning blue,
My toe penetrates rubbery imperfection.
I used to pray to resole you.
Ach, du.

Kate Cooper

SONNET TO AN ANASAZI SLIPPER

(based on William Shakespeare's
'Shall I Compare Thee to a Summer's Day?')

───◆●◆───

SHALL I compare thee to a worn PA?
Thou art more sticky and more sensitive:
Rough grit doth scrape and scratch and fray,
And other boots last for all too short a date:
Sometime too hot the eye of heaven shines,
And then even is thy sure friction dimm'd,
And even Stealth from fair sometime declines,
By wear or nature's hazards to thy rubber trimm'd:
But thy eternal prowess shall not fade,
Nor lose possession of that style thou showest,
Nor shall Boreal brag thou wand'rest in his shade,
When after innumerable climbs thy fit doth goest,
   So long as men can climb up to 7c,
   So long lives this and this gives life to thee.

Marc Chrysanthou

THE SICK ROPE

(based on William Blake's 'The Sick Rose')

O ROPE, thou art sick!
The invisible tear
From a careless knife,
In the gear hold-all,

Has found out thy core
Of perlon joy,
And this dark secret gash
Does thy life destroy.

Marc Chrysanthou

THE ROPE NOT TAKEN
(based on Robert Frost's 'The Road Not Taken')

Two ropes diverged (unlike the book said they should),
And sorry I could not drag up both –
Fearing dreadful rope drag – long I stood,
Then sent down one as safe as I could
Like a snake into the undergrowth;

Then I took the other, safest of the pair,
Having perhaps the better gear chain,
Because it ran truer, and wanted wear;
Though as for that, the sharp edges there
Had worn them really about the same.

On that wall my strength ebbed away –
I saw no means of turning back –
Two ropes diverged (not as they should), and I –
I chose the one less snaggled by
Doubt, and when I fell it made all the difference.

Marc Chrysanthou

FORGIVEN
(based on A.A. Milne's 'Forgiven')

I HAD a little Camalot, so that Cammy was his name.
And I called him 'my life-saver' and he answered just the same.
I clipped him to my harness, and I climbed throughout the day ...

And I couldn't get the bugger out
Yes I couldn't get the bugger out
She went and over cammed it
And it stays there to this day.

My partner said she didn't mean it,
And I never said she did,
She said she just got frantic
And she shoved it in
Too deep.

She said that she was sorry, but it's difficult to place
A perfect four cam unit when you're clinging to the face.
She said that she was sorry, and I really mustn't mind,
As there's lots of other abandoned gear which she's certain we could find,
If we looked about on Stanage on the routes beginners climb.
We'd get another Camalot and mark it up as mine.

We went to all the places where a piece would often stick.
With butter knives and engine oil to make the placement slick,
And as I strained against the rock, and I felt the crowbar bend,
A ton of rock went groundwards and I got another Friend.

And my partner's very sorry too, for you-know-what she did.
And she's wrapping brand new marking tape very tightly round the clip
So She and Me are friends ... because it's difficult to place,
An expensive four cam unit when you're clinging to the face.

Paul Saunders

WIRES
(based on Spike Milligan's 'Rain')

———◆●◆———

THERE are cracks in the rocks
Where the wires go in
The cracks are small
That's why they make them thin.

Nick Alcock

THE POISON ROCK 3
(based on William Blake's 'A Poison Tree')

———◆●◆———

I WAS angry with my Friend:
I scoured my rack, my wrath did end.
I was angry with my pro:
I told it not, my wrath did grow.

And I water'd it in fears,
With my sweat and with my tears;
And it gleamed a steely smile,
And mocked me with deceitful wiles.

And it rocked both left and right,
Till it loosed and took to flight;
And my pro began to shine,
For it knew that Death was mine,

And demon-like my strength it stole
Till my last gear ripped from a hole:
And later it was glad to see
My corpse outstretch'd upon the scree.

Marc Chrysanthou

MOST EVERYWHERE
(based on AA Milne's 'Market Square')

———◆●◆———

I HAD quickdraws
Bright new quickdraws
I took my quickdraws
To the Peak District fair
I wanted a sports route
A three-star sports route
I looked for a sports route
'Most everywhere

For I went to a crag called Stanage Plantation
(Loads of lovely E grades at Stanage plantation)
Have you got a sports route, coz I don't like E grades
But they hadn't got a sports route, not anywhere there

I had quickdraws
Bright new quickdraws
I took my quickdraws
To the Peak District fair
I did want a sports route
A nice safe sports route
And I looked for a sports route
'Most everywhere

And I went to a crag which was called Burbage North
(Loads of short trad climbs at Burbage North)
Have you got a sports route, coz I don't like trad climbs
But they hadn't got a sports route, not anywhere there

I had quickdraws
Bright new quickdraws
I took my quickdraws
To the Peak District fair
I was finding my sports route
I do like sports routes

And I looked for a sports route
'Most everywhere

I went to a crag which they called Curbar Edge
Lots of routes to solo at Curbar Edge
Could I try a sports route, coz I'm rubbish at soloing
But they hadn't got a sports route, not anywhere there

I had no gear
No, I hadn't got no gear
So I didn't go down to the Peak District fair
But I walked to the Quarry
The old crumbly quarry
And I saw sports routes
'Most everywhere!

So I'm sorry for the people who like to go soloing
I'm sorry for the people who climb short trad routes
I'm sorry for the people who climb scary E grades
Coz they haven't got sports routes, not anywhere there!

(the contents of this poem do not necessarily represent the views of the author!)

Amanda James

HE WISHES FOR THE MATS OF HEAVEN
(based on W.B. Yeats' 'He Wishes for the Cloths of Heaven')

HAD I the heavens' upholstered mats,
Enwrought with stitching and filled with foam,
The blue and the black and the red mats,
S7, Metollius or Franklin Drop Zone,
I would spread my mats under your feet:
But I, being poor, have only my dreams;
I have spread my dreams under your feet;
Fall softly, because you fall on my dreams.

Marc Chrysanthou

THE CLIMBER WHO HAS NO TOES

(based on Edward Lear's 'The Pobble Who Has No Toes')

THE climber who has no toes
Had once as many as we;
When they said 'Some day you may lose them all'; –
He replied, – 'Not an alpinist like me!'
And he grabbed his axe, and his crampons sharp,
To the Eigerwand in winter he was bound,
A very fine ascent he made, but I'm afraid
His toes were never found.

Nick Alcock

We've all had one, a day out in the mountains that puts to shame the wanderings of Odysseus or the adventures of Lawrence of Arabia: walking for hours trying to find a pub in Wales that's open on Sundays or going up Snowdon by train on a particularly windy day. Viewed later from the comfort of a hot bath they become epic narratives of the triumph of the human spirit over formidable adversity, and can be embellished and lengthened to send the most attentive listener to sleep.

THE MARMOT AND THE ALPINIST
(based on Lewis Carroll's 'The Walrus and the Carpenter')

THE sun was shining on the peak,
  Shining with all his might:
He did his very best to make
  The snow slopes smooth and bright –
And this was odd, because it was
  The middle of the night.

The moon was shining sulkily,
  Because she thought the sun
Had got no business to be there
  After the day was done –
'It's very rude of him,' she said,
  'To come and spoil the fun!'

The snow was white as white could be,
  The rock was dry as dry.
You could not see a cloud, because
  No cloud was in the sky:
No birds were flying overhead –
  There were no birds to fly.

The Marmot and the Alpinist
  Were walking far below;
They wept like anything to see
  Such quantities of snow:
'If this were only cleared away,
  It would set my heart aglow!'

'If seven guides with seven spades
  Shovelled for half a year.
Do you suppose,' the Marmot said,
  'That they could get it clear?'
'I doubt it,' said the Alpinist,
  And shed a bitter tear.

'O Freshers, come and walk with us!'
    The Marmot did implore.
'A pleasant walk, a pleasant talk,
    And peaks to bag galore:
To give a rope to each of you,
    We can at least take four.'

Last year's Freshers looked at him,
    But never a word they said:
Last year's Freshers winked their eyes,
    And shook their heavy heads –
Meaning to say they did not choose
    To leave their squalid beds.

 But four young Freshers hurried up,
    All eager for the treat:
Their duvets brushed, their faces washed,
    Their boots were clean and neat –
This wasn't odd, because they'd only
    Worn them in the street.

Four other Freshers followed them,
    And more beyond all hope;
And thick and fast they came at last –
    The pair could scarcely cope –
All hopping off the minibus,
    And tying on the rope.

The Marmot and the Alpinist
    Walked up a mile or so,
And then they rested on a rock
    Conveniently low:
And all the little Freshers stood
    And waited in a row.

'The time has come,' the Marmot said,
    'To talk of many things:
Of crampons – pegs – and belay plates –

Of harnesses – and slings –
And why you can't climb up the rope –
And why a rockfall stings.'

'But wait a bit,' the Freshers cried,
  'Before we have our chat;
For some of us are out of breath,
  And all of us are fat!'
'No hurry!' said the Alpinist.
  They thanked him much for that.

'A deep crevasse,' the Marmot said,
  'Is what we chiefly need:
A weakened snow-bridge too besides
  Is very good indeed –
Now if you're ready, Freshers dear,
  We can begin the deed.'

'Don't drop us please!' the Freshers cried,
  Turning a little blue.
'After such kindness, that would be
  A dismal thing to do!'
'The night is fine,' the Marmot said.
  'Do you admire the view?

'It was so kind of you to come!
  And you are very nice!'
The Alpinist said nothing but
  'Belay us to the ice:
Make sure those ice screws are secure –
  And tie us to them twice!'

'It seems a shame,' the Marmot said,
  'To play them such a trick,
After we've brought them out so far,
  And made them trot so quick!'
The Alpinist said nothing but
  'The snow here is too thick!'

'I weep for you,' the Marmot said:
  'I deeply sympathize.'
With sobs and tears he sorted out
  Those of the largest size,
Holding his pocket-handkerchief
  Before his streaming eyes.

'O Freshers,' said the Alpinist,
  'You've had a pleasant run!
Shall we be trotting home again?'
  But answer came there none –
And this was scarcely odd, because
  They'd pushed down every one.

Helen Oughton

GROOVED ARÊTE? V DIFF AT BEST!
(based on Wilfred Owen's 'Dulce Et Decorum Est')

BENT double, like old beggars under rucksacks,
Knock-kneed, coughing like hags, we cursed through sludge,
Till on Tryfan's north ridge we turned our backs,
And towards our distant rest began to trudge.
Both marched asleep. One had lost his boots,
But limped on, blood-shod. Both went lame, both whined;
Drunk with fatigue; deaf even to the hoots
Of an eagle owl calling softly behind.

Fags! Fags! Quick, boys! – An ecstasy of fumbling,
Sucking the noxious fumes sublime,
But hark! someone's yelling out and calling,
And shouting 'Mountain rescue!' time after time …
On through the misty rains and thick black night,
I realise it's me! We go on walking.

In recurring dreams since that fateful plight,
I relive the thrutching, flailing, falling.

If in some smothering dreams you too could take
The sight of 'Hang on, Daz! I'm struggle-ing!'
As The Knight's Move reared its polished face,
And he sought to get some protection in;
If you could hear, at every jolt, the curses
Come gargling from his cigarette-corrupted lungs;
Obscenities like 'Wanker! Bugger, it's no good!'
As a wild, implausible leap made us bite our tongues, –
My friend, you would not tell with such high zest
To climbers ardent for some multipitch glory,
The old Lie: 'Grooved Arete? V Diff at best –
There's pro and gear, don't worry!'

Darren Jackson and Marc Chrysanthou

ALBERT AND THE CARTHORSE

(based on Marriot Edgar and Stanley Holloway's 'Albert and the Lion')

THERE'S a famed gritstone crag known as Stanage,
As is noted for fresh air and fun,
And Mr and Mrs Ramsbottom,
Went there wi' young Albert, their son.

A fine little climber, were Albert,
In his Stone Monkey vest, quite a swell,
He'd a new pair of boots, and a harness,
The finest that Cotswold could sell.

Well, he didn't think much of the gritstone,
The holds were all rounded and small,
There were no gear, and some chance of falling,
In fact, nothing to laugh at, at all.

So seeking for further amusement,
And for something exciting to do,
He went to climb Helfenstein's Struggle,
That's a Diff (though it should be E2!)

Well he shinned up the bottom right easy,
Like a monkey goes straight up a pole,
But the upper part gets a bit narrow,
And it swallowed the little lad whole.

Well, he twisted and turned in his prison,
And he tried to get out with an udge,
But no matter how hard he wriggled,
The poor little lad couldn't budge.

Now Ma, who had seen the occurrence,
And not knowing what to do next,
She said, 'Pa, yon climb's ate our Albert!'
And Father said, 'Ee, I am vexed!'

Well, they couldn't extract little Albert,
By tugging the end of his line;
Then someone said, 'Call Mountain Rescue',
So they went and they rang 999.

Now the Rescue weren't too sympathetic,
When they heard about Albert's mishap,
In fact, most of them fell about laughing,
And one fellow started to clap.

'Oh, won't you come quickly?' cried Mother,
Who was now in a bit of a state.
'Nay, there's no point in coming this weekend,
Not until the young lad's lost some weight!'

So it wasn't until the next weekend
That the Rescue Team turned out in force,
With lots of cold beer and jam butties,
And a long piece of rope – and a horse!

Now, the name of the carthorse were Wallace,
He were worth every penny o' t' hire:
He'd won every prize going for pulling,
He were best horse in all Derbyshire.

So they tied end o' t' rope onto Wallace,
And he pulled like he'd sommat to prove,
But in spite of his very best efforts,
Young Albert, he still couldn't move.

Wallace pulled, and he kept on pulling,
But it seemed they were right out of luck,
'Til Wallace were nearly exhausted,
And the Team Leader muttered, 'Oh, bother!'

Then he gathered the Team all around him,
And said, 'Now lads, come listen to me,
Someone must go down to Buxton,
And come straight back here wi' Plan B.

When the man came back, some hours later,
They all knew this would be their last hope,
He'd a bucket of green Fairy Liquid,
Mixed with old engine oil, and soap.

They emptied the bucket on Albert,
And they greased him from bottom to top,
Then they tied the rope back onto Wallace,
And the Team Leader shouted, 'Gee-up!'

Then Wallace, he strained every sinew,
This were no Sunday afternoon stroll!
With a noise like an elephant farting,
Young Albert popped out of his hole.

He flew through the air, quite a distance,
And came down to land on some grass,
With nothing to show for his mishap,
But a nasty black bruise on his elbow.

Then Albert he turned to his mother,
Who was still looking rather perplexed,
And said 'Eh, Mother, that were right smashing,
Can I do Right Unconquerable next?'

At that Mother got proper blazing!
'This climbing's too dangerous a game!
Next weekend, we're going back to Blackpool –
You can play with that lion again!'

Howard Jones

TYGER ON THE EIGER
(based on William Blake's 'The Tyger')

———◆●◆———

EIGER! Eiger! burning bright
Like a monster cloaked in white,
What mere mortal hand and eye
Could tame thy fierce geology?

To thy citadel of sighs,
Comes a man with fiery eyes;
On what wings dare he aspire?
What brave man dare risk thy ire?

What broad shoulders, & what art,
Could cross the icefields at thy heart?
And when thy heart begins to beat,
What firm hand? & what sure feet?

With Thor-like hammer and cool brain,
The Hinterstoisser's ghost is slain;
With pterodactyl in sure grasp,
He dares thy deadly terrors clasp.

When The Spider spews its spears,
And shatters helmets, inflames fears;
Did he smile with dreadful glee?
Did the man from Grindelwald climb thee?

Eiger! Eiger! burning bright,
Like a monster cloaked in white,
What mere mortal hand and eye
Dared tame thy fierce geology?

Marc Chrysanthou

KUBLA KHAN
(based on Samuel Taylor Coleridge's 'Kubla Khan')

IN Argentière did Kubla Khan
A lengthy Alpine trip decree:
Where Arve, the schisty river ran
Through caverns measureless to man
   Down to Chamonix.
So twice five yards of sloping ground
With tents and mats were girdled round:
And here were climbers fat with freeze-dried meals,
Who lay neath the washing-line-bearing tree;
And they ate oatcakes ancient as the hills
On which grew spots of greenery.

But oh! that deep romantic cavern which slanted
Down the seracs athwart a snow-bridge cover!
A savage place! as holy and enchanted
As e'er beneath a waning moon was haunted
By barmaid wailing for her Preston lover!
And from this chasm, with ceaseless turmoil babbling,
A man with Ron Hill pants was scrabbling,
His mighty axes momently were thrust:
And planted in the glacier's crust.
Then slid he like a Benzedrine snail,
Down the flanks of the glacier so pale;
And 'mid these dancing rocks at once and ever
Plunged, yetis and all, into the silty river.
Five miles floundering like a cork on the sea
Through floods and torrents our fated hero swam,
Then reached that tavern heaven-sent to man,
As he sank in tumult in the Bar Nationale:
And 'mid this tumult Kubla heard from the Bar
Froggie voices proffering Vladivar!

Tom Chamberlain

THE CLIMBS THEY ARE A-CHANGIN'

Things are not as they once were. Things weren't even as they were when they were what they once were (see Nostalgia). However, I'm sure that the crags weren't white when I started climbing, that we didn't have to pay to park our cars when we went to The Roaches, we didn't have to queue to get on Valkyrie, women weren't allowed to lead unless supervised by their husbands, and no-one kicked up much of a fuss if old Frank gave you a shoulder on Crack & Corner. Last week they hung him ...

THEY FUCK YOU UP, THOSE WHO CLIMB TRAD
(based on Philip Larkin's 'They fuck you up, your mum and dad')

THEY fuck you up, those who climb trad.
　They may not mean to, but they do.
They fill you with the faults they have
　And add some extra, just for you.

But they were fucked up in their turn
　By fools despising bolts on routes,
Who half the time were soppy-stern
　And half in one another's boots.

Man hands on misery to man.
　It deepens like a coastal shelf.
Get out as early as you can,
　Boulder, toprope, please yourself.

Darren Jackson

CHANGING THE GRADES
(based on AA Milne's 'Buckingham Palace')

THEY'RE changing the grades, and I think it's callous,
V this, Font that, it's done with malice.
Alice is working on 6c, 7a,
'That's not a Font grade, no way!'
Says Alice.

They're changing the grades, and I think it's callous,
Headpointed, toproped, soloed with a mattress.
We saw a young man strapped to a mat,
'See how his Mum has knitted his hat,'
Says Alice.

They're changing the grades, and I think it's callous,
The rocks are covered in plaster of Paris,
We looked in our book for a clean-looking crack,
'They've given the guidebook writer the sack,'
Says Alice.

They're changing the grades, and I think it's callous,
Downgraded routes, it's a poisoned chalice.
'Do you think Mark Vallance knows all about me?'
'Sure to, dear, but it's time for tea,'
Says Alice.

Nick Alcock

COME FRIENDLY BOMBS

(based on John Betjeman's 'Come friendly bombs and fall on Slough')

COME, friendly bombs, and fall on Stanage!
It isn't fit for climbers now,
There's top ropers and bouldering,
And chalk covers every prow!

Nick Alcock

I WANDERED ONCE UP TO HEN CLOUD

(based on William Wordsworth's 'I wandered lonely as a cloud')

I WANDER'D once up to Hen Cloud
That floats on high o'er Staffordshire's hills,
When all at once I saw a crowd,
A host of toproping imbeciles;
Upon the crag, beneath the trees
Flailing and thrutching in the breeze.

Continuous as the stars that shine
And twinkle on the Milky Way,
They stretch'd in never-ending line
From each and every parking bay:
Ten thousand saw I at a glance
Striding out with determined stance.

I geared up, picked my route, advanced; but they
Hogged the sparkling lines in glee: –
A Trad Climber could not but dismay,
In such unethical company:
I gazed – and gazed – but only thought
'Bastards! My winter training brought to nought.'

For oft, when on my couch I lie
In vacant or in pensive mood,
They flash upon that inward eye
Which is the bliss of solitude;
And then my heart with displeasure fills,
And curses toproping imbeciles.

Darren Jackson

THE CLIMBS THEY ARE A-CHANGIN'
(based on Bob Dylan's 'The Times They Are a-Changin')

COME gather round, people
Wherever you climb
For I'd have you take heed
And attend to my rhyme
You know, I've been climbing a very long time
And I've seen a few things,
I am claimin'
But the sport's a lot different
From when I began
For the climbs they are a-changin'

Now when most of the routes
Were first done around here
They were climbed in EBs
And with bugger-all gear
But today we can stitch them
All up without fear
And in 5.10s the friction's amazin'
But although they've got easier
They've gone up a grade
For the climbs they are a-changin'

And in the old days
It was all very clear
To go the gym, well,
You never would hear
And they climbed on a diet
Of ciggies and beer
But nowadays everyone's trainin'
And they'd rather climb plastic
Than go to a crag
For the climbs they are a-changin'

Now some people claim
That delight can be found
In climbing the boulders
That are scattered around
Though they climb 7a
They don't get off the ground
And they've got their own system of gradin'
And they carry a mattress
Instead of a rope
For the climbs they are a-changin'

Come bumblies and fogeys
Throughout the land
If you don't criticise
Then they won't understand
The chippers and bolters
Are beyond your command
The old ways are rapidly fadin'
And Ethics is where
You'll find Southend-on-Sea
For the climbs they are a-changin'

Howard Jones

I Love to Go a-Bouldering

There was a time when bouldering was considered a trivial pursuit –
at best, training for the high mountains. How things have changed!
Now the smaller and more insignificant the lump of rock the better.
Now there isn't a stone in existence that doesn't feature in some
bouldering guide. Even the tiniest pebble can provide a severe challenge
if tackled from a lying-down, upside-down, underground start.

BRAD PIT
(based on Elizabeth Barrett Browning's 'How Do I Love Thee?')

How do I climb thee?! Let me count the ways.
I'll climb thee by a stretch and lunge to the height
My arms can reach, when the jug that's out of sight
Will feel my fingers slot into place.
I'll climb thee by means of chalk-drenched layaways,
Most sly heel and toe-hooks and finger-might.
I'll climb thee nearly, till the moves are right;
I'll climb thee purely, so none can turn from praise.
I'll climb thee with the passion of rock's muse
With my bold dreams, and with my childlike faith.
I'll climb thee with a love I seemed to lose
With repeated falls, – I love with the breath,
Sweat, tears, of all my life! – and, if Rock choose,
I *shall* climb thee before I enter unto death!

Marc Chrysanthou

So We'll Go No More a-Bould'ring
(based on George Gordon, Lord Byron's 'So We'll Go No More a-Roamin' …')

So we'll go no more a-bould'ring
So late into the night,
Though the will be ne'er unyielding,
And the urge be still as bright.

For the rock outwears the man,
And cruel Time wears out the best,
And rock athletes themselves must pause,
And seek their well-earned rest.

Though the day was made for climbing,
And the dusk gathers too soon,
You and me'll go no more a-bould'ring,
Nor the likes of Ben Moon.

Marc Chrysanthou

BOULDERING DAYS

(based on Robert Louis Stevenson's 'Windy Nights')

———◆●◆———

WHENEVER Ben Moon's runners are set,
Whenever the rock is high,
All day long and move by move,
There's a pause to shake out and dry.
Late in the night when his wires are out,
Why does he boulder and boulder about?
Whenever his spotters are crying aloud,
And it's past the time for tea,
Down on the headwall, steep and cold,
Another new route goes free.
Down on the boulders he goes, and then
Slaps for the break, *again and again.*

Nick Alcock

STOPPING BY ROCKS ON A SNOWY EVENING

(based on Robert Frost's 'Stopping by Woods on a Snowy Evening')

WHOSE woods these are I think I know.
His house is in the village though;
He will not see me stopping here,
To boulder as it starts to snow.

The passing cars must think it queer
To stop without a farmhouse near.
Between the woods and frozen lake
The darkest evening of the year.

I give my chalk-warmed hands a shake,
And squeak my boots (so no mistake).
The only other sound the leap
Of soul to rock and hand on flake.

The woods are lovely, dark and bleak
But I have challenges to seek,
And moves to make before I sleep,
And moves to make before I sleep.

Marc Chrysanthou and Nick Alcock

ROMANCE ON THE ROCKS

*It is no accident that Heathcliff and Cathy's romance is set amidst
the wild moors. There is something about high places that stimulates
in vulnerable spirits the madness known as love. Unfortunately,
the nearness of precipitous cliffs often results in such romances
proving short-lived.*

TANGLES
(based on Bob Dylan's 'Tangled up in Blue')

EARLY one morning the sun was shining,
I was laying in bed
Thinking of all the routes I'd done
Running them round in my head.
Memories of days together,
Some of them were rough
I never did like the long run outs,
The gear was never big enough.
And I was standing by the side of the slab
Rain falling on my shoes
Heading up for the big lead,
Lord knows I've paid some dues getting through
Tangled up in blue.

The crags were dark when we first met
Soon to be lit by the sun
I started out with a jam, I guess,
But I used a little too much force.
We climbed that route as high as we could
Abandoned it out left
Split up on a dark sad night
Both agreeing it was best.
She turned round to look at me
As I was climbing down
I heard her say over my shoulder,
'We'll meet again some day it's true,'
Tangled up in blue.

I had a trip to the American rocks
Climbing hard for a spell
But I never did push it very much
And one day my leader fell.

So I drifted back to the climbs at home
Where at least I knew the score
Climbing for a while down south
To the sound of the ocean's roar.
But all the time I was alone,
The past was close behind,
I'd done a lot of hard routes
But she'd never escaped my mind, and I just grew
Tangled up in blue.

She was climbing in an indoor place,
And I stopped in for a look,
I just kept looking at her style and grace
As deep inside I shook.
And later as the crowd thinned out,
I was about to start a climb
She was standing there on a belay
Said to me 'Don't I know your name?'
I muttered something underneath my breath
She studied the lines on my face,
I must admit I felt a little uneasy
When she took off my climbing shoe
Tangled up in blue.

She chalked up, and offered me the rope
'I thought you'd never say hello,' she said
'I'd given up all hope'.
Then she opened up an old guidebook,
And handed it to me
Written by an Italian climber
From the last century.
And every one of those climbs I knew
And every move stood out
Pouring off of every page
Like they were written in my soul, from me to you
Tangled up in blue.

I lived with them in Llanberis
In a basement down the stairs,
There was climbing on the slate by day
And revolution in the air.
Then she started climbing alone
And something inside of me died.
I sold all the gear I owned
And froze up inside.
And finally when the fun ran out
I became withdrawn,
The only thing I knew how to do
Was to keep on, keeping on the way I knew
Tangled up in blue.

So now I'm going back again,
I've got to get back to the climbs
All the routes I used to know
They're an illusion to me now.
Some are steep
Some are steep and cold
Don't know how it all got started,
I don't know if they've changed the grades
But me, I'm still on the rock
Heading for another crag
We always did feel the same
We just saw it from a different point of view,
Tangled up in blue.

Nick Alcock

THE OWL AND THE CRAGRAT
(based on Edward Lear's 'The Owl and the Pussy-cat')

THE Owl and the Cragrat went to Wales
   In a beautiful lime-green Jag.
They took some 'stickies', and plenty of biccies
   Wrapped up in an old chalkbag.
The Owl looked up to the cliffs above,
   And sang to a small guitar,
'O lovely Ratty! O Ratty, my love,
What a beautiful Ratty you are,
     You are, You are!
What a beautiful Ratty you are!'

Ratty said to the Owl, 'You elegant fowl!
   You're so cute, with you I'll elope!
But let's try Cloggy! before it gets foggy:
   But what shall we do for a rope?'
They clambered away, for the rest of the day,
   To the stance where the Whortle-tree grows,
And there in a hood a Grey Badger stood,
With a rope wrapped around his toes,
     His toes, His toes!
With a rope wrapped around his toes.

'Gray Ruff, are you willing to sell for one shilling
   Your rope?' Said the Badger, 'I will.'
So they took it away, and climbed Shrike all the way
   Till they could see to the top of the hill.
They followed the track to Yr Wyddfa's shack,
   Where they were wed by a grey-tailed Buffoon;
And hand in hand they danced to a band
   Till they floated up in a balloon,
     Balloon, Balloon,
They floated up in a balloon.

Marc Chrysanthou

ODE TO A NIGHT IN A GALE
(based on John Keats' 'Ode to a Nightingale')

MY tent shakes, and a drowsy numbness pains
　My sense, from all the cider that I've drunk.
My mind is in turmoil about the drains,
　One minute past, and I'll be sunk:
'Tis my bladder, not my happy lot,
　To leave the tent and all happiness, –
　　To venture to that Dryad of the trees,
　　　In some malodorous plot
Of dark and gloom, and sheep shit numberless,
　Without a torch in winter, ill at ease.

O, for a down jacket! That hath been
　Warm'd a long age by love within my berth,
Smelling of perfume and wintergreen,
　Deep Heat, Chanel, and sunburnt mirth!
O for ablutions from the warm South,
　Full of true Andrex and Nivea cream,
　　With hot running water and a shower trim,
　　　And a brush to clean my mouth;
That I may pee, and leave the world unseen,
　And fade back to my tent in forest dim.

Fade far away, dissolve, and quite forget
　What those cosy in the pubs have never known,
The weariness, the stench, and tummy upset
　Here, where I sit and hear my fellow climbers groan;
Where socks grow stale, and optimism dies,
　Where but to think is to be full of sorrow
　　And hollow-eyed despairs;
　　Where Beauty shows off her lustrous thighs
　　　From a *Playboy* that we chanc'd to borrow.

All day! All day! Without a cup of tea,
　Nor Walkman nor e'en a pack of cards

Trapp'd like a clueless thing of Destiny,
  Who my dull brain perplexes and retards:
Already hungry! Endless is the night
    Unhaply none of us has a mobile phone,
      So there's no chips or curried takeaways;
        And here there is no light
Save what from heaven is with the breezes blown
    Through endless driving rain and choking, foggy haze.

I cannot feel my half-frostbitten feet,
  Only the immense weight of gloom upon my brow,
But, in the becalmèd darkness, I retreat
  To where my fev'rish mind allows
A glass of whiskey, and a plate tall-piled
  With roast beef, served with the finest wine;
    Follow'd by biscuits and crumbly cheese;
      And The Green Man's finest mild,
    Then a perfumed bath, with bubbles divine,
      Soap-scented with honey from murmuring bees.

Wand'ring I listen; and for many a time
  I have been mad in love with peaceful Geoff,
Call'd him soft names in many a muted rhyme,
  To take into my heart his manly breath;
Now more than ever seems it time to try,
  To reach under his duvet with no shame,
    While he is snoring upon his back so broad
      And I'm in ecstasy!
Hitherto my love had anguished in vain –
  Till now my love was only known to God.

'Thou wast not born for Geoff, infernal cur!'
  So came vibrations from the eiderdown;
The voice I heard give me a fright was her,
  Geoff's fiancée, who slowed us as we hurried down:
The hag, the self-sure wench who lost the path
  Through the mist – 'Well done, Ruth!' – when, sick for home,

We stood in tears amid the alien zawn;
   The dame that oft-times hath
Charm'd Geoff's Rohan breeches open, for his foam,
   On perilous climbs, as I looked down forlorn.

Forlorn! the very word is like a bell
   To toll me back from cruel dreams to myself!
Adieu! I unzip the flap, lurch into Hell,
   As the downpour makes treach'rous the shelf.
Adieu! adieu! Geoff's memory fades
   I crawl through meadows, vault a wild stream,
     Up the hillside; and now 'tis very steep
       Till the next valley-glades:
   Was it a vision, or a drunken dream?
     Long fled is my Vango: – do I wake or sleep?

Marc Chrysanthou and Nick Alcock

LA BELLE DAME SANS MERCI

(based on John Keats' 'La Belle Dame Sans Merci')

―――――⋅◆●◆⋅―――――

O WHAT can ail thee, Bulging Arms,
Alone and palely loitering?
The Edge has closed down for the night,
And The Foundry's emptying?

O what can ail thee, Bulging Arms!
So haggard and so woe-begone?
Thy boulderer's chalkbag's nigh full,
And thy 5.10s still on.

I see the sweat thick on thy brow
With anguish moist and fever dew,
And on thy cheeks a gritstone rash
Fast withereth too.

'I met a climber in The Queen's,
Full beautiful – a faery's child,
Her hair was long, her foot was light,
And her eyes were wild.

I made a garland for her head,
And bracelets too, from Rizla wraps;
She look'd at me as we did eat,
Our warm chip baps.

I set her on my Honda twin,
And nothing else saw all day long,
For sidelong would she lean, and sing
A gritstone song.

She found me arêtes hellish steep,
Roofs so high, and slabs so smooth.
And she promised me her lovely charms –
If I could their worst subdue.

Victorious! She took me to her cave,
And there she lay and sigh'd full sore,
And there I shut her wild wild eyes
With kisses four.

And there she lullèd me asleep,
And there I dream'd – ah! woe betide! –
The cruellest dream I ever dream'd
On the cold hill side.

I saw pale youths in baggy clothes,
Pale boulderers, death-pale were they all;
They cried – 'La Belle Dame sans Merci
Hath thee in thrall!'

I saw their starved lips in the gloam,
With horrid warning gapèd wide,
And I awoke and found me here,
On the cold hill side.

And this is why I sojourn here,
Alone and palely loitering,
Though The Edge has shut down for the night,
And The Foundry's emptying.'

Marc Chrysanthou

THE PASS (OR THE ROAD THAT WINDS ITS WAY)
(based on Rudyard Kipling's 'Mandalay')

BY the Vaynol arms, Nant Peris, in the early afternoon,
There's a bored young lass a-waitin' for a lift arranged at noon;
The sun is on the high crags, she is keen to be away,
But 'er partner's stuck in traffic on the by-pass near Conwy.
'I did 'ope to climb today,
On Craig Ddu just down the way,
Which I'm told is in condition
On this sunny summer's day.'
On the road that winds its way,
Through the cliffs where climbers play,
An' the traffic roars like thunder up the Pass from far-away!

'Er Goretex coat were yeller and 'er flowin' 'air was wild,
The time was gettin' on an' she were gettin' riled,
As she stood there with 'er mobile a whackin' out a text,
You could tell from 'er expression that she were mighty vexed!
But she was out of signal range –
Which really isn't strange,
'Cos it's 'ard to get a message through
This lofty mountain range!
On the road that winds its way …

T'was arranged last week at North Face and confirmed again last night,
They planned the details on the phone, the forecast were quite bright.
She was in Llanberis an' 'e in Liverpool,
'E said it was an 'our's drive, she thought 'the bloody fool!'
It's an 'oliday weekend,
And it no use to pretend
That you can travel swiftly with caravans a'plenty,
An' roadworks on each bend!
On the road that winds its way …
'I am sick of wastin' time on a partner far away,
An' a park'n'ride that doesn't seem to work Bank 'Oliday!
I'll find an 'andy bunk'ouse where I can ditch my kit,

Then wander down to Cromlech and boulder for a bit.'
With that the young lass sigh'd,
And fish'd out a dog-ear'd guide;
And perused it as she calmly
Stuck 'er thumb out for a ride!
On the road that winds its way …

Oh leave me in North Wales where one can climb all day,
Workin' up a mighty 'unger for a meal at Pete's Café.
For the Vaynol Arms is callin' me to sink another pint,
And plan multi-pitch adventures beneath the star-fleck'd night!
So no rain tonight I pray,
On the rugged rocks so grey;
For Craig Ddu is in condition,
I 'ear the local climbers say.
On the road that winds its way,
Through the cliffs where climbers play
And the traffic roars like thunder up the Pass from far away!

Duncan Bourne

CHANSON D'AMOUR D'UN GRIMPEUR
English translation: 'A Groper's Lust Thong'
(based on John Betjeman's 'The Subaltern's Love-song')

—◆●◆—

MADAME C. Destivelle, Madame C. Destivelle,
Full-lipp'd and firm-hipp'd, *vous êtes très belle!*
What strenuous problems you mastered at *'Bleau,*
High on *L'Eléphant* – *Quelle* view from below!

F7, V11, oh 36C!
The grace of *un oiseau, vous êtes très jolie.*
Avec un je ne sais quoi, vous avez grimpé so well,
I am weak from your loveliness, Madame Destivelle.

Madame C. Destivelle, Madame C. Destivelle,
How mad I am, sad I am, glad that I fell
Into your arms as you sensed my *faiblesse,*
Oh, my raven-haired beauty, *j'adore la caress!*

The scent of Chanel and the sound of Piaf,
From a Paris hotel room as you laze in your bath,
While I trudge up from Ogwen, sighing *'J'en ai marre',*
Dans mes rêves we're in heaven, *Catherine et moi!*

Marc Chrysanthou

GENIUS LOCI

Guidebooks can describe routes in terms of length, severity and specific challenges. They cannot, however, convey that indefinable, ineffable sense of atmosphere – the Spirit of Place. Whose soul could fail to be stirred by a mist-wreathed cwm or the sublime immensity of the Eiger's North Face? But for real atmosphere, a night at a deserted climbing wall is unbeatable – cold, dark, spooky (tip: in future, always ensure wall staff know everyone has vacated the cave feature).

INDOOR HAVEN

(based on Gerard Manley Hopkins' 'Heaven Haven')

———◆•◆———

A bum takes to the wall

I HAVE desired to go
    Where cams not fail,
To walls where flies no sharp and sided hail
    And a few wallies go.

And I have asked to be
    Where no storms come,
Where the sweat smell is in the rafters rum,
    And without the sting of reality.

Gordon Stainforth

WALL GOING

(based on Philip Larkin's 'Church Going')

———◆•◆———

ONCE I'm sure there's nowt much going on
I step inside, holding my Adidas bag zipped shut.
Another wall: mats, ropes, fake stone,
And little holds; sprawlings of boulderers, pumped
For Sunday, clownish now; some roofs and stuff
Up at the gnarly end; the tall, steep lead wall;
And a tense, sweaty, musclebound silence,
Brewed Rockworks™ knows how long. Ron-Hill-less, I take off
My polar fleece in awkward reverence.

Look upward, imagine that I'm back at Font.
From where I stand, the routes look almost new –
Cleaned, or reset? Squawk Dunn would know: I don't.
Flaunting my pectorals, I pursue a few
Meandering, vague traverses, then pronounce
'Here endeth the attempt' more loudly than I'd meant.
The echoes snigger briefly. Back at the door,
One final look, I admire a stylish wench,
Reflect her face was not worth stopping for.

Gordon Stainforth and Marc Chrysanthou

UPON LEEDS WALL STAIRS
(based on William Wordsworth's 'Composed Upon Westminster Bridge')

LEEDS has not anything to show more fair:
Dull would he be of soul who could pass by
A sight so touching in its majesty:
This wall now doth, like a garment, wear

The beauty of the morning; silent, bare,
Jugs, slopers, crimps, features, and side-pulls lie
Open unto my hands and to my eye;
All bright and colourful in the chalkless air.

Never did sun more beautifully steep
In his first splendour, valley, rock, or hill;
Ne'er saw I, never felt, a calm so deep!

Al Manson hoovereth at his own sweet will:
Dear God! the very barrels seem asleep;
And all those mighty ropes are lying still!

Kate Cooper

HALFWAY DOWN
(based on A.A.Milne's 'Halfway Down the Stairs')

———◆•◆———

HALFWAY down the crag is a rock where I sit.
There isn't any other rock quite like it.
I'm not at the bottom, I'm not at the top.
So this is the rock where I always stop.

Halfway up the crag isn't up and isn't down.
It isn't on a scary route, it isn't in the town.
All kind of funny thoughts go running round my head.
It isn't really anywhere, it's somewhere else instead.

Amanda James

PETE'S EATS
(based on Emily Dickinson's 'Wild Nights ... Wild Nights!')

———◆•◆———

WILD Nights ... Wild Nights!
A full Pint of Tea!
Pete's Eats will be
Our luxury!

Futile ... the Winds ...
To a climber Fed and Warm ...
Full of All Day Special Breakfast ...
Thus our Hearts full of Calm.

It's wet in Llanberis ...
Ah, but the Treats!
Might I but stay ... Tonight ...
At Pete's!

Kate Cooper

(Dis)Organised Climbing

*Climbers are by nature pack animals. They herd together like sheep —
forming clubs, bouldering in groups. Gang warfare is rife, and that
freak of nature, the solitary climber, can often be found wandering
the moors with his eyes pecked out by more gregarious souls.*

ANARCHY IN THE B.M.C.
(based on J. Rotten, S.Jones, G. Matlock and P. Cook's 'Anarchy in the UK')

————◆●◆————

RIGHT! NOW! ha ha ha ha ha

I am an antichrist
I am an anarchist
Don't know what I want but
I know how to get it
I wanna destroy the block vote cos I

I want BMC anarchy!
No dogsbody

Anarchy for the B.M.C. it's coming sometime and maybe
You fat old clubs have had your day cos
your future dream is an insurance scheme cos I

I want BMC anarchy!
In the city

How many ways to get what you want
I use the best I use the rest
I use the enemy I use anarchy cos I

I want BMC anarchy!
THE ONLY WAY TO BE!

Is this the FRCC
Or is this the AMA
Or is this the CC
I thought it was the BMC or just
another climbing club
another bunch of old guard tossers

I wanna be an anarchist
Oh what a name
Get PISSED DESTROY !

Kate Cooper

THE MARCH OF THE TRAD BRIGADE

(based on Alfred, Lord Tennyson's 'The Charge of the Light Brigade')

I

HALF a lead, half a lead,
  Half a lead onward,
All in the valley of Neath
  Climbed the six punters.
'Forward, the Trad Brigade!
'I'll mantle for the break!' one said;
High in the valley of Neath
  Climbed the helmeted warriors.

II

'Forward, the Trad Brigade!'
Was this a man dismay'd?
Not tho' the climber knew
  That he'd been sandbagged:
His not to make reply,
His not to reason why,
His but to do and die:
High in the valley of Neath
  Climbed the hobnailed blunderer.

III

No gear to right of him,
No gear to left of him,
No gear in front of him
  Breathless and pump'd;
Swearing with slip and smear,
Boldly runout as well,
Into the jaws of Death,
Into the mouth of Hell
  Climbed the self-belayed shunter.

IV

Slipped from the route so bare,
Flash'd as he turn'd in air,
Scaring the watchers there,
Charging downwards, while
  All his mates wonder'd:
Plunged past the belay point
Right thro' his line he broke;
Screaming and cussing
Reel'd from the impact stroke
  Shatter'd and sunder'd.
Not to come back, oh no,
  Not the *Classic Rock* bumbly.

V

Who can his glory fade?
The onsight attempt he made!
  All his mates sicken'd.
Honour the climb he made!
Honour the Trad Brigade,
  All brave V Diff hunters!

Paul Saunders, Marc Chrysanthou
and Gordon Stainforth

There are four seasons of the year. For real climbers there is only one –
Summer. Of course, there are idiots who climb in Spring and
Autumn as well. There are even bearded types who don weird apparel
and climb in Winter's snow and ice – utterly mad, all of them.

THE CLIMBER
(based on Lewis Carroll's 'Humpty Dumpty's Song')

IN winter, when the crags are white,
I climb the ice with sheer delight –
In spring, when routes are slightly green,
I'll try my luck on the boulder scene.
In summer, when the days are long,
I'll climb big walls, for now I'm strong:
In autumn, when the leaves are brown,
I'll stick to grit without a frown.

Amanda James

THE CLIMBER'S TALE
(based on William Chaucer's Prologue to 'The Canterbury Tales')

WHAN that Aprill with his shoures soote
The droghte of March hath perced to the roote,
And fromme the Ynland Revenue we here
To welcome inne the new fynancial yere;
Then alle the clymbers they have hadde enough
Of clymbinge onne the artyficial stuffe,
Atte the Foundry or the North West Face,
And they are all fulle sicke of Rope Race.
But soone, whyle alle the people lye aslepe,
Bright Phoebus forward in his course doth leepe
To summon inne the British Summer Time,
And itte is then thatte folkes go forth too clymbe;
From far and near they go on pilgrymage
To Stoneye Mideltonne and Hathersage,
Whyle somme do turn their faces further west,
To Cloggy, Tryfan, Idwal and the reste.
But tho the shoures swete falle on the toun,
Upon the hilles itte generally pysseth down.

A manne there was, in Manchester did dwelle,
Who liked to clymb upon the rocks fulle welle,
This manne, of whom I telle to you my tale,
His clymbinge loved, but better loved hys ale,
For even tho the sunne was past the prime,
He stille would notte bestir himself to clymbe;
Butte satte alle inne the tavern supping beere.
He had no monnaie left to buy his geere,
Some tatty slynges, a rope fro longe ygo,
Thre Rocks he hadde, foure hexes, and namo,
Butte tho of clymbinge geere he sore did lacke,
A vow he made that he'd clymbe Kern Knottes Crack.
And so onne daie he walked up to the route,
Altho he was as sober as a newt,
And tho he hadde a bellyful of beere,
He started on the clymb without a fere;
Butte when he cam unto the tricky bitte,
He could notte fynd a piece of geere to fitte,
And he was so befuddled by the booze
That hys balaunce he very soone did lose.
And so before too longe itte came to passe,
This manne fell doune, and landed on his arse.
He lowd did groan as onne the grownd he layed,
And piteouslie did crye out for first ayd;
He loudlie called for somebodie to come,
And putte some stickinge plaster onne hys bumme.
And before verie longe, I'm gladde to saye,
The Mountayne Rescue carryed him awaye.

The moral, if a moral there shold bee,
Iffe you wold clymbe, then always sticke to tea;
For iffe onne bere or whisky you shold sup,
You may fynd thatte your lucke is alle used up.
But iffe you cannot do without the pubbe,
Thenne joyn Innominata Mountain Clubbe.

Howard Jones

NESTING OF THE GEAR
(based on W.H. Auden's 'Stop All the Clocks')

———— ◆●◆ ————

STORE all the chocks, and the Franklin Drop Zone,
Prevent the krabs from rusting, wrap them in foam.
Silence reigns on the edges, fingers too numb,
Bring out the photos, let the memories come.

Let hardier climbers to the ice-cliffs head
Scrabbling up gullies as this 'tiger' lies in bed,
Put a pull-up bar in the garage or in the attic above,
Let the cagouled morons don their Dachstein gloves.

It was my *Gritstone East,* my *Gritstone West,*
My play after work, my Sunday test,
My *High,* my *Rocktalk,* my beer, my song;
I thought summer would last forever: I was wrong.

The guidebooks are not wanted now: rest every one;
Pack up the ropes, now the season's done;
Pore over the videos, and train on the wood.
Let the project patiently wait until the daffodils bud.

Marc Chrysanthou

ODE TO A WINTER CLIMBER
(based on Robbie Burns' 'To a Mouse')

BIG, hairy, smelly beastie,
Where are ye gaun sae hastie!
Thou need na start, nane will chase thee,
Tae yer hill,
Tha route is yours lane, it's virgin tae:
Go, tak thy adrenalin pill!

The hills is empty, nane is there,
So thee can enjoy, wi time tae spare
The red deer an' white mountain hare,
Afore they startle,
When thy reach's snow, ice and mair,
Thou'll ken thy's mortal!

Pitch after pitch, upwards ye'll go
'Til thou's hangin' on a dice, an it's thy throw
Ane mair heave wi axes, a bawl, and lo
'Tis a braw sight!
The summit, 'tis cover'd in snow,
On this glorious, moonlit night.

Descent is slow on legs sae wearie,
Adrenalin gone noo, vision's blearie,
Energy sapped, but thou's content and happy,
No longer feart;
Warm feelin returns, thou'll soon be cosy,
Thee, whae have the mountains sae close tae heart.

Anita Laidlaw

CLIMBING IN A GRITSTONE WONDERLAND
(based on R. Smith and F. Bernard's 'Walking in a Winter Wonderland')

HEXES ring
are you listening
on your rack
nuts are glistening
A beautiful sight
we're happy and bright
climbing in a gritstone wonderland

Gone away is the Ouzel
we can jam and bamboozle
A spectating throng
as we go along
climbing in a Stanage wonderland

On the crag top we can build a belay
shouting 'Climb when ready' at the ground
He'll say: 'Are you tied in?'
We'll say: 'No man!'
'And if you take a lob
then I'll fall down'

Later on
we'll perspire
as we smear up Messiah
And dangle afraid
on routes that Don made
climbing in a Burbage wonderland

In the meadow we can find a boulder
and attempt to start it sitting down
We'll use lots of chalk until our shoulder
pops and leaves us writhing on the ground

Heaven knows
ain't it thrilling
Though your tips take a killing
We'll frolic and play
the whole of the day
climbing in a gritstone wonderland

Climbing in a gritstone wonderland
Climbing in a gritstone wonderland

Darren Jackson

THE ICE CLIMBING SONG
(based on Nat King Cole's 'The Christmas Song' written by
Mel Torme and Robert Walls)

————◆◉◆————

WALLNUTS hanging on a frozen wire,
Jack Frost nipping at your nose.
Shiny axes ringing out like a choir,
And folks dressed up like Eskimos.
Everybody knows,
A cornice and some crispy snow
Help to make the season bright.
Camalots, cammed as far as they go,
Will find it hard to grip tonight.
You know that winter's on its way:
You're looking out for icy gullies for your play.
And every lad and lass is gonna try,
To keep their feet, and pray not to fly.
And so I'm offering this simple phrase
To kids from 1 to 92,
Although it's been said many times, many ways:
Happy Crimpfest to you.

Darren Jackson

Let us first sing of one who should be knighted – Mighty Joe (The Baron) – then go on to jeer at those who should be benighted (on a ledge three inches wide, 10,000ft up on some sheer North Wall, without a drill, chisel hammer or teddy bear for company).

ODE TO JOE BROWN
(based on William Blake's 'Jerusalem')

———◆●◆———

AND did Joe's feet in 'ancient' time
   Walk upon England's moorlands green?
And was the holy jamming god
   On England's rough steep grit cracks seen?

And though a mountaineer sublime,
   Who shone in Karakoram hills,
He carved a true hard man's career
   Amid the scars of mines and mills.

Sing me of Joe, master of old!
   Sing me of Joe, gritstone messiah!
Sing me of Joe! Of climbs so bold!
   Sing me of Joe, ascending higher!

He did not cease from mental strife,
   Nor did the skin stay on his hands,
He put up routes that we still fear:
   He's England's greatest mountain man.

Marc Chrysanthou

THE CRAVEN
(based on Edgar Allan Poe's 'The Raven')

ONCE upon some gritstone dreary, I inched my way up, weak and weary,
Up a slab so steep and smeary, the famous Tody's Wall –
While I fumbled, blindly slapping, suddenly I heard a rapping,
As of someone gently tapping – tapping a bolt into the wall.
'Tis some blasphemer,' I muttered, 'tapping a bolt into the wall –
     Damn his soul for evermore!'

But although my rage grew stronger, I could levitate no longer,
'Sir,' said I, 'your craven action I would usually deplore;
But the fact is I am slipping, and cold fear is strongly gripping,
So I welcome now your rat-a-tat-tat-ing a bolt into the wall!'
And he caught the rope I flung him; clipped it to the bolt above him: –
     Praise be his name evermore!

Alison Bond and Marc Chrysanthou

MacChipperty the Mystery Chipper

(based on TS Eliot's 'Macavity: the Mystery Cat')

MacChipperty's a Mystery Man: he's climbing's Hidden Sore –
For he's the phantom chipper who can defy the Law.
He's the bafflement of Purity, the Ethics Squad's despair:
For when they reach the scene of crime – *MacChipperty's not there!*

MacChipperty, MacChipperty, there's no one like MacChipperty,
He's broken every climbing law, he takes a lot of liberties.
His powers of alteration would make a sculptor stare,
And when you reach the scene of crime – *MacChipperty's not there!*
You may seek him in the quarry, you may look up in the air –
But I tell you once and once again, *MacChipperty's not there!*

MacChipperty's a clever guy, he's very tall and thin;
You would know him if you saw him, for his eyes are sunken in.
His brow is deeply lined in thought, his chisel's highly honed;
His fleece is dusty from neglect, his beard is all uncombed.
He sways his head from side to side, with movements like a snake;
And when he thinks you're safe asleep, he's always wide awake.

MacChipperty, MacChipperty, there's no one like MacChipperty,
He's a fiend in human shape, bane of the grit fraternity.
You may meet him at The Bridestones, or Brimham's Dancing Bear –
But when a crime's discovered, then *MacChipperty's not there!*

He's outwardly respectable (I know he cheats at cards),
And his chiselmarks are not found in any files of Scotland Yard's.
And when a climb's been sculpted, or the guidebook's grades are rifled,
Or when a hold goes missing, or a last great line's been stifled,
Or the Dawes' line's been stolen so there's no End of the Affair –
Ay, there's the wonder of the thing! *MacChipperty's not there!*

MacChipperty, MacChipperty, there's no one like MacChipperty,
There never was a man of such deceitful serendipity.
He always has an alibi, and one or two to spare:
Whatever time the deed took place – *MacChipperty wasn't there!*

And they say that all the Men whose wicked deeds are widely known,
(I might mention Peter Livesey, a Man who 'nail-brushed' stone)
Are nothing more than second to the Man who all the time
Kills climbs for future generations: the Napoleon of Crime!

MacChipperty, MacChipperty, there's no one like MacChipperty,
He's a fiend in human shape, a cur of great iniquity.
You may meet him in a quarry, you may see him on Thin Air –
But when a crime's discovered, then *MacChipperty's never there!*

MacChipperty, MacChipperty, MacChipperty,
When a hold's been added, then – MACCHIPPERTY'S NOT THERE!
MacChipperty's not there!

Marc Chrysanthou

THE RIME OF THE ANCIENT GRITSTONER
(based on Samuel Taylor Coleridge's 'The Rime of the Ancient Mariner')

PART I

IT is an ancient Gritstoner,
And he stoppeth one of three.
'By thy long grey beard and glittering eye,
Now wherefore stopp'st thou me?

The BMC's doors are open'd wide,
It is the area meeting;
The guests are met, the agenda set:
May'st hear the chairman's greeting.'

He holds him with his skinny hand,
'There was a crag,' quoth he.
'Hold off! unhand me, grey-beard loon!'
Eftsoons his hand dropt he.

He holds him with his glittering eye –
The BMC Guest stood still,
And listens like a three years' child:
The Climber hath his will.

The BMC Guest sat on a stone:
He cannot choose but hear;
And thus spake on that ancient man,
The tweed-clad Mountaineer.

'The crag they brush'd, the lichen clear'd,
Merrily did they sup
Below the crag, below the hill,
Below the gritstone top.

The Sun came up upon the cheats
As they hatch'd their 'noble' plans,
Boulders to be 'sent' and first ascents
Awaited every man.

But being in a drunken way,
They didn't set off 'till noon –'
The BMC Guest here beat his breast,
For he heard the loud buffoon

Of a Chairman clearing out his throat:
'Time for a vote' said he;
And the BMC Guest heard the answ'ring cries
Of the climbing fraternity.

The BMC Guest he beat his breast,
Yet he cannot choose but hear;
And thus spake on that ancient Man,
The bright-eyed old Gritstoner.

'And now the STORM-BLAST scotch'd their plans
With rain both hard and long:
And once again denied them rock,
Which they'd waited for so long.

With sloping holds and jutting prow,
The crag did tempt them so.
But Lo! I came to life again
Though dead eighty years ago!

I stalk'd them like a shadowy foe,
And forward bent my head,
The rain drove hard, loud roared the blast,
As upwards the bould'rers led.

At length they cross'd a young Ouzel:
Through the fog it came;
And ramblers and park wardens,
Stopp'd them climbing in its name.

It ate their food ere they could eat,
And round and round it flew.
And though they eye'd the virgin lines,
The wardens would not let them through!

As good south winds did dry the crag;
The Ouzel it did follow.
And every day, for food or play,
Came to the climbers' hollow.

'Till when at last they gain'd access,
Impatient for their claim;
And fearful of the stronger teams,
They sought their climb to tame.'

'God save thee, ancient Gritstoner!
From the cheats that plague thee thus! –
A deed so evil ... With their cold chisels
They *chipped* the buttress thus.'

PART II

'The Sun now rose upon the cheats
To cast an accusing eye,
And my voice was heard, as if from the rock,
"All chippers must surely die!"

For they had done an hellish thing,
And it would work 'em woe:
I took stock that they'd smash'd the rock
With every hammer blow.
"Ah wretches!" said I, "the rock to slay
With every hammer blow!"

The foul adze slew, the grit dust flew,
Some pockets follow'd free.
They were the first that ever durst
Say "Ethics are not for me!"

Down dropt the adze, the chips dropt down,
'Twas as sad as sad could be;
And they did think only to break
To have a cup of tea!

Slaughter, slaughter, everywhere,
As the holds they tried to link;
Slaughter, slaughter, everywhere,
For many a pock and dink.

The very crag did rot: O Christ!
That ever this should be!
Yea, these slimy beings did crawl with legs
Upon my grave and me.'

And in their dreams assured they were
Of the Spirit that plagued them so:
For they had heard Jim Puttrell's voice
A-cursing them below.

Then one with clumsy arrogance,
Struck he another blow,
A boulder splinter'd from the route.
And hurtled down below ...

It struck his partners senseless,
They tumbled from their place,
The rock swept down to smother them,
Leaving him stranded 'pon the face.

Ah! well a-day! What evil looks
Had he for one so young!
Instead of a medal, a bevell'd Chisel
About his neck was hung!

PART III

'He faced the greasy climb. Each hold
Was drench'd, nor any crevice dry.
A greasy climb! a greasy climb!
Nor any crevice dry.
Then, looking westward, he beheld
My spirit with his eye.

At first he seem'd a mite perplex'd,
As if he'd seen a mist ;
He moved and moved, he rubb'd his eyes,
As though he were 'bit piss'd.

A speck, a mist, a shape, he wist!
And still I near'd and near'd:
And as I swoop'd down like a kite,
I smiled and laugh'd and jeer'd.

With hope all gone, with black heart baked,
He could not shriek nor wail;
Through utter fear all still he stood!
I bit his arm, I suck'd the blood,

His spirit dipp'd; his heart gush'd out:
His one life sensed the dark;
With a far-heard whisper, o'er the moor,
He rued his chisell'd mark.

Four times fifty mercy pleas,
And a thousand sighs and groans,
With heavy thump, a hopeless lump,
He dropped down like a stone.

Before his soul didst from him fly –
His face grew pale and ill.
His empty soul began to cry,
Like the buzz of his own rock-drill!

"I fear thee, ancient Gritstoner!
I fear thy skinny hand!
For thou art J.W. Puttrell,
Noblest of a noble band.

I fear thee and thy unwav'ring eye,
And thy skinny hand so brown –
Fear not. I'll never chip again – "
Then his spirit ceased to sound.

Alone, alone, all, all alone,
On an E10 he'd made E3!
And may a saint take pity on
His soul in agony.

His chipping crew, so covetous!
They too all dead did lie:
Only their ropes and shiny slings
Lived on; and so did I.

I look'd upon the bloodèd scree,
And drew my eyes away;
I look'd upon the bloodèd ledge,
To where the dead man lay.

Ethics! They are a noble thing
Infringed from pole to pole!
To the pioneers be Praise forever!
Socks and plimsolls in all weather,
My iron dwelt in my soul.

I pass, like night, from this sad land;
I lose my power of speech;
The Godless chipper's face I see,
I know in Hell he must hear me:
To him my tale I teach.

Farewell, farewell! but this I tell
To thee, thou BMC Guest!
He climbeth well, who careth well
For the crags which we've been blest.

He climbeth best, who loveth best
All rocks both great and small;
For the Rock God who loveth us,
He made and loveth all.'

The Gritstoner, whose eye is bright,
Whose beard with age is hoar,
Is gone: and now the BMC Rep
Turn'd from the Committee Room's door.

He went like one that hath been stunn'd,
And is of sense reborn:
A nobler and a wiser man
He rose the morrow morn.

Paul Saunders, Marc Chrysanthou
and Gordon Stainforth

OSSIE MANDIAS

(based on Percy Bysshe Shelley's 'Ozymandias')

I MET a climber from Gritstone East land
Who said: Two vast and holdless prows of stone
Stand on the moors. Near them, lies a hand,
Beside a shattered body, whose bones,
And wrinkled lips, and sneer of cold command,
Tell that its owner met a harsh, violent end,
At the hands of a mob who didn't agree
With one who sought to add holds and nature bend,
With hammer and chisel and a brush of wire –
And chiselled on the rocks these words you'll see:
'My name is Ossie Mandias, the Bolt-gun Messiah:
Look upon my climbs, ye Mighty, and despair!'
Nothing beside remains. Round the decay
Of those brute-scarred prows, boundless and bare
The lone and level moors stretch far away.

Marc Chrysanthou

Nostalgia

There was a golden age of climbing when the crags were deserted, and heroic types called Godfrey soloed in tweeds and hob-nailed boots to rescue petticoated damsels in distress on mountain ledges. Very Difficult climbs were the absolute limit of climbing prowess, and it never rained. I know ... I was there.

DESTRUCTION
(based on John Betjeman's 'Norfolk')

How did the Devil come? When first attack?
These crags recall lost innocence,
The years fall off and find me climbing back
On moss covered stone and across the cracks
Up this same route, where thirty years ago
My father climbed above me, calm and slow.

I used to fill my hand with sorrel seeds
And shower him from the tops of waterfalls;
I used to pull the rope and watch him smile
To make him hurry up those sunny walls
Of granite, grass and ledges, till here
Our route's end and belay would appear.

How did the Devil come? When first attack?
The crags are still the same, though now I know
Many have destroyed it. Time bring back
The rapturous ignorance of long ago,
The Peace, before the dreadful onslaught starts,
Of unkept promises and broken hearts.

Nick Alcock

THE OLD CLIMBER

(based on Lewis Carroll's 'You are old, Father William')

———— ◆●◆ ————

'YOU are old, Father William,' the young man said,
   'And your Ron Hills are so passé;
And what's that thing you've got on your head –
   Do you think, at your age, it looks fey?'

'In my youth,' Father William replied to his son,
   'I climbed every route in the Pass;
From Cenotaph Corner to Route Number One,
   Even though they were covered in grass.'

'You are old' said the youth, 'as I mentioned before,
   And have grown most uncommonly fat;
Yet you swung on that jug twenty foot from the floor –
   Pray, what is the reason for that?'

'In my youth,' said the sage, as he shook his grey locks,
   'Our boots were not very sticky,
I climbed the hardest routes in my socks –
   Try it yourself, it's quite tricky.'

'You are old,' said the youth, 'one would hardly suppose
   That your balance was as steady as ever;
Yet in the rain, you soloed the Nose –
   What made you so awfully clever?'

'In my youth,' said his father, 'I climbed all right
   With only slings and stones for protection,
And most of the routes I climbed on sight,
   In the end I achieved perfection.'

'You are old,' said the youth, 'and your arms are too weak,
   For anything tougher than drinking;
Yet last year you ticked most of the Peak,
   Please let me in on your thinking?'

'I have answered three questions, and that is enough,'
  Said his father, 'My advice isn't free!
Do you think I can listen all day to such stuff?
  It's like a meeting of the BMC!'

Nick Alcock

FOLLOWER
(based on Seamus Heaney's 'Follower')

My father climbed up at Laddow,
On boulders ribbed like giant shells strung.
A man-plough ploughing rock furrows,
His torso strained at his catlike lunge.

An expert. He would take to wing
Skimming wet slabs in woollen sock.
The crags rolled over, surrendering –
At the headwall, with scarce a look.

Or pause, his stretching frame reached round
And out sprang a hand. His mind
Arrowed and angled, then unwound,
Mapping the furrows, till entwined.

I stumbled in his hob-nailed wake,
Fell sometimes on the polished flake;
Sometimes he rode me on his back
Dipping and rising with his grace.

I wanted to emulate his flow,
To train my eye, stiffen my arm.
All I ever did was follow
On his trusty rope, safe from harm.

I was a nuisance, slipping, falling,
Yapping always. But today
It is my father who keeps stumbling
Behind me, and will not go away.

Marc Chrysanthou

INTIMATIONS OF MORTALITY

The skeletons of sheep littering our hillsides remind us that the life of man is also a nasty, brutish, short existence. There is no Friend 7, no 'bomber' gear, no toprope to prevent us from taking that great leap of doom into the abyss of nothingness. But, look on the bright side: if grit really is 'God's Own Rock', what great climbing there must be in Heaven ...

To a Coy Buttress

(based on Andrew Marvell's 'To His Coy Mistress')

———— ❖ ————

HAD we but the Weather, and the Time,
This stern Sequence would be mine.
I would sit down even, do it that way
Or give it best and return another Day;
Down by the *shaded Churnet* side
I should'st Bunter pebbles find; or by and by
Vital Tendons flex and train. I should
Strive secretly and strain on Wood;
And my Frustration and Ambition hide
Till Publication of the Avon Guide.

My lactate Tolerance should grow
Mighty, and my twitch fibres more slow.
An hundred Circuits should go to raise
Aerobic Fitness, and over many Days;
Two hundred Pull-ups daily and the rest,
(and Results full flaunted in low cut Vest)
Structured Training to every part,
And a Monitor to check my Heart.
For, to achieve this well-honed State,
I would have it beat at lower rate.

But at my back I always hear
My Spotter's crude and callous Jeer;
And all around I only see
Blank and stark Impossibility.
No purchase have my Fingers found,
Nor pliant mat ease my fall to ground,
Curse echoing strong; then shall Others try
That over-brush'd Rugosity,
And so all my Efforts come to nought,
And all high Resolve and Dreams mere Thought.
The Gym's a hard and heartless place,
But only those who work find grace.

Now therefore, while some dregs of youth
Remain in my limbs, though scarce enough
And while the leaning Wall inspires
Every sinew with at least some Fire,
Now let us sport us while we may;

And now, perhaps more like careful Sloth,
Than the subtle Squirrel of our youth,
Let not languish this slow-chapp'd Power.
Let us don our beanie, cast off else all
Save scant fleece-lined Bag to hold chalk Ball;
And tear our Knuckles with rough Grit
Leap at Life or what remains of it.
Thus, though our Project may ne'er be done
We may, yet, climb toward the Sun.

Dave Garnett

A GRITSTONE CRACK

(based on Alfred Lord Tennyson's 'Crossing the Bar')

SUNSET and evening star,
  And one last route for me!
And may there be no moaning at the bar,
  Can all the drinks be free?

But the chosen route is a gritstone crack,
  The holds unchalked and green,
The cams are stacked around my back,
  I think you know the scene.

Twilight and, Oh dear,
  I've got a jam, I can't let go!
To reach the pro, I'll have to get a smear,
  But there's lichen on my toe;

For tho' the darkness falls on Time and Place
  The rope might hold me far,
I hope to see my Maker face to face
  When I lean across the bar.

Nick Alcock

LET ME DIE A HARD MAN'S DEATH

(based on Roger McGough's 'Let Me Die a Youngman's Death')

LET me die a hard man's death
not a serene dreaming of Pete's Eats
safe asleep at home death
nor a tripping-on-my-laces
falling off Crib Goch death

When I'm 73
& cruising Painted Rumour
may I be suddenly surprised
by a loose and brittle flake
as I start to cross the roof
and fall flat on my face

Or when I'm 91
with silver hair
& soloing Hubble for a dare
may rival climbers
with high-powered boltguns shoot me down
& leave me dead and bolted to the ground

Or when I'm 104
& bouldering at Sennen
may I hear a mother cry
as her child is washed away
dive in and rescue little Ray
then have a heart attack
as my good deed she seeks to repay.

Let me die a hard man's death
not a falling from my attic
storing away my ropes and gear death
not a hit by a stray rock sunbathing
'what a stupid way to go' death.

Marc Chrysanthou

In Memoriam

Wherever we climb, we are surrounded by ghosts. Some of these spirits are friendly ghosts – protecting us from harm. Of course, there are also black-robed faceless evil demons on day-release from the flames of Hell (but that's enough about topropers ...)

Strange Meeting With Mallory

(based on Wilfred Owen's 'Strange Meeting')

It seemed that from the icefall I escaped
Down some vast ice tunnel, long since scooped
Through granites which tectonic shifts had groined.
Yet also there enfeebled climbers groaned,
Too trapped in sleep or death to be bestirred.
Then, as I probed them, one sprang up, and stared
With brotherly recognition in tired eyes,
Lifting regretful hands, as if to bless.
By his lithe stance against that Stygian wall, –
By his strange smile I knew his name full well.
With a thousand pains that legend's face was grained;
Beside him Irvine writhed upon the ground,
Now, sadly slumped, George Mallory made moan.
'Strange friend,' I said, 'here is no cause to mourn.'
'None,' said Mallory, 'save the undone years,
The fruitlessness. Whatever hope is yours,
Was my life also; I dared to dream wild
Of climbing the highest mountain in the world,
Chomolungma! Goddess with snowy hair
Possessed my hopes and dreams at every hour,
As still it breathes weird life into me here.
When we set forth, dear Odell smiled and laughed,
Now weeping at my loss is all that's left.
The dream must die now as my fate is told,
'Mallory and Irvine', the myth distilled.
Now men come to retrace the dream left spoiled
Or, disabused, toil vainly, their egos spilled –
Their death-slides swifter than the snow tigress,
Yet none will break faith with this cruel Empress.
Chomolungma unclimbed, I loved her mystery,
Everest unclimbed, I sought its mastery:
To kiss the grail of the mountaineering world
Aloft a citadel so sternly walled.
Then, when my triumph snagged on careless heels,

I plunged headlong down yellow-banded walls:
Irvine's frail youth dragged down too deep for taint;
He always poured his spirit without stint,
Until cruel wounds struck with success set fair
The Second Step tamed, the summit not far.
I am your spirit-brother, my friend.
I saw you stumble in the dark: the way you frowned
Yesterday with fear as you slipped and fell.
You grappled; but cold hands could not halt your fall.
Let us sleep now ...'

Marc Chrysanthou

A NEGLIGENT SECOND REMEMBERS
(based on Christina Georgina Rossetti's 'Remember')

REMEMBER Steve when he's gone astray,
    Gone far away from the line he plann'd;
    When, above the wind, he can't understand
Your panick'd call, 'the rope's run out all the way'.
Remember Steve when no more can he say
    'Watch me here, it's a beast this overhang;
    Only remember, his life's in your hands,
It will be late to counsel then or pray.
Yet if you should forget Steve for a while,
    And afterwards remember, do not grieve:
    For if he falls as your mind's on leave,
    And your ATC's as much help as a brillo pad –
Better by far forget his blood and bile
    Than that you should remember and feel bad.

Marc Chrysanthou

A Scottish Tragedy
(based on William Shakespeare's Macbeth, Act V, Sc 5)

—————————◆●◆—————————

'SHE should have told her father:
It was too hard a climb for such a nerd –
To grovel, and to grovel, and to grovel,
Creeping his sweaty way from b'lay to b'lay
To the last smelly hold of that sordid climb;
But all her nut belays frighteningly pulled
Away to leave a bloody mess! Out, out, weak anchors!
She was but a gawping saddo, a pisspoor belayer,
Who fussed and frittered an hour upon her stance,
Till he was heard no more....' This is a tale
Told by a bigot, full of loudmouthed fury,
Signifying much gin.

Gordon Stainforth

Not Soaring but Falling
(based on Stevie Smith's 'Not Waving but Drowning')

—————————◆●◆—————————

NOBODY heard him, the dead man,
But still he lay moaning:
I was much further up than you thought
And not soaring but falling.

Poor chap, he always loved climbing
And now he's dead
It must have been too hard for him his nerve gave way,
They said.

Oh, no no no, it was too hard always
(Still the dead one lay moaning)
I was much too high up all my life
And not soaring but falling.

Marc Chrysanthou

DO NOT STAND NEAR THE SLOTH AND WEEP

(based on 'Do Not Stand at My Grave and Weep', attributed to Mary Frye)

———◆●◆———

Do not stand near The Sloth and weep,
I am not there, I do not sleep.

I am the chilling wind that blows.
I am the green-streaked slab below.
I am the sunlight on the moor.

I am the fear of a dropped quickdraw.

When you rack up beneath the roof,
I am the energy of youth,
The soaring wing of a curved arête,
The drifting smoke from a cigarette.

Do not stand near The Sloth and weep.
I am not there, I do not sleep.
Do not stand at my grave and bawl.
I am not there, I did not fall.

Marc Chrysanthou

LIGHTS OUT ...

*Time to take off the rucksack, gather around the campfire,
break out the beer and sing ...*

No Way!
(based on the lyrics to Frank Sinatra's song, 'My Way'
by Paul Anka and Gilles Thibault)

---◆•◆---

AND now, the end is near;
And so we face the past; uncertain.
The cigar smoke's so thick in here,
It's time we cleaned the club hut's curtains.

We've lived a life that's dull,
We've seen slide-shows of every high way;
But when we met real rock
We all said 'No Way!'

Weird pranks, we've pulled a few;
When Alec tried that bold 'extension'.
We laughed as he clutched the branch
I'd sawn half-through with due attention.

We've read Ed's climbing book;
Imagined every step of Norgay,
But when The Big One called
We all said 'No Way!'

Yes, there were times, I'm sure we knew
When we set off without a clue.
But through it all, when there was doubt,
We turned and ran or abseiled out.
We faked it all and still stood tall;
We just said 'No Way!'

We've snubbed, we've cast aside.
We've dumped our share of red-socked losers.
Except the ones who like to lead
Who tow us up climbs that elude us.

To think we fooled them all,
We never climbed – 'cept on a nice day,
And as for ice and snow,
We just said 'No way!'

For what is a man, what has he got?
If not his life, then not a lot!
We'd rather be someone who breathes;
Than cold and dead in the Pyrenees.
We never go where danger goes –
We just say 'No Way!'

Marc Chrysanthou

Index of Titles

Right! NOW! ha ha ha ha ha, 107

Safe in the magic of the crag, 20
Shall I compare thee to a worn PA? 49
'She should have told her father', 148
So we'll go no more a-bould'ring, 81
Store all the chocks, and the Franklin
    Drop Zone, 114
Sunset and evening star, 142

The chief defect of Henry King, 32
The climber who has no toes, 57
The man stood on the belay ledge, 43
The Owl and the Cragrat went to
    Wales, 89
The sun was shining on the peak, 60
There are cracks in the rocks, 53
There's a famed gritstone crag known as
    Stanage, 65
They fuck you up, those who climb
    trad, 72
They're changing the grades, and I think
    it's callous, 73
To smear or not to smear: that is the
    question, 34
'Twas chossy and the slimy rock, 29
Two ropes diverged (unlike the book said
    they should), 51

Wallnuts hanging on a frozen wire, 117
Whan that Aprill with his shoures
    soote, 112
Whenever Ben Moon's runners are
    set, 82
Who will go climb with Fergus now, 42
Whose woods these are I think I
    know, 83
Wild Nights ... Wild Nights! 103
Wobbliest of knees, my left knee now, 28

'You are old, Father William,' the young
    man said, 135
You do not do, you do not do, 48